KU-360-658

WAL 83

Slipping the Tugs

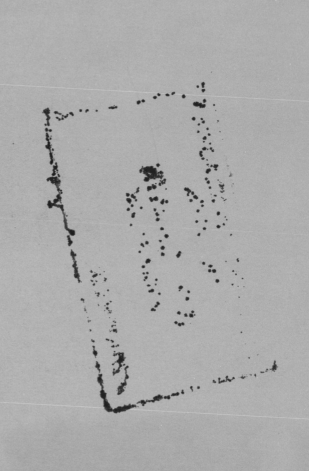

SLIPPING THE TUGS

poems by
Maurice Rutherford

NORTH EAST LINCOLNSHIRE LIBRARIES WITHDRAWN FROM STOCK AUTHORISED:

LINCOLNSHIRE AND HUMBERSIDE ARTS 1982

Lincolnshire and Humberside Arts
St. Hugh's, 23 Newport, Lincoln LN1 3DN

HUMBERSIDE
LIBRARIES
GRIMSBY GROUP

BAR	IMM
BT	LAC
CEN	MOB
CLP	NUN
GOX	SCA
GT	WAL 5/91
HUM	WIL
	YAR

© Maurice Rutherford 1982

ISBN 0 906465 24 9
ISSN 0140-8550

HUMBERSIDE LIBRARIES

GRIMSBY DIVISION LIBRARIES

Group G

Class 821.914

ISBN

GRIMSBY GROUP LIBRARIES

Acc. No. H1566400

Plessey No.

BRANCH COPY

B25346405 8

Designed and Illustrated by Ron Harrison

Printed in
Great Britain by David Green Printers Limited, Kettering

CONTENTS

Acknowledgements

Acknowledgements and thanks are due to the editors of the following publications in which some of these poems first appeared: *Envoi; Here Now; Iron; Lincolnshire Life; Poetry Nottingham; Proof; Thirty '82; To Build A Bridge.* 'Going Back', 'Sonnet: Through Mother's Eyes', and 'The Quiet Men' were awarded Merits in Lake Aske Memorial Open Competitions; 'Slate' was highly commended in the Surrey Open Poetry Competition, 1981; 'Heinz Gropsmeyer' was a Diploma winner in the Scottish Open Poetry Competition, 1982; 'Irreverence' was broadcast on BBC Radio 3 *Poetry Now.*

INTRODUCTION

As Maurice Rutherford's editor for this collection of his verse, I have, in a sense, travelled with him many times. For 'Slipping the Tugs' is very much about a journey. Chronologically, the events of his poems move from Hull and the North Bank of the Humber where he was born and grew up, to the South Bank where he now lives. But there is a far greater distance to be travelled than that recently foreshortened, both in reality and in the mind, by the Humber Bridge. Time and again, there is a conflict between his sense of belonging and his restlessness, and so the poetic attention shifts from the local and immediate to more uncertain (but for various reasons compelling) regions. But movement does not exist only in his imagination; he has been uprooted in his lifetime, most violently by the brutality of war, and perhaps his most powerful poetic statement derives from this experience. What survived war and upheaval, to be expressed in many of these poems, was a fresh and sensuous response to the natural world, a sensitivity to what Louis MacNeice called "the drunkenness of things being various".

I have enjoyed the trip. And before the tugs are finally slipped, I would metaphorically break a celebratory bottle against these ample bows, and recommend a journey at the end of which is wisdom of that kind discovered by the Greek poet, Cavafy, who wrote of another odyssey:

> *". . . if you find her poor, Ithaka hasn't deceived you.*
> *So wise have you become, of such experience,*
> *that already you'll have understood what these Ithakas mean."*

Allen Prowle

"from the names, and the things no less"

for
Olive, Ian and Jean

POEM ON SATURDAY

Outside my window, a linnet on the laburnum
shows poetry to the other birds, preens,
stutters its wings and corrugates away
across the lawn, and the nest of words
I am waiting to hatch goes cold.

Yesterday, as from the office window I watched
a vessel leave the lockpits, outward bound
for Genoa, slipping the tugs from the task in hand,
my feet were treading Italian ground
before the Humber had healed in her wake.

I knew, once, a tall school window high above
the tiers of desks where, in carbolic air,
peas imprisoned in a jar strove for the sky
and begged me join in the climb to a place where
every day was Saturday and Saturday was Christmas.

THE CYCLE

I was tall enough then to stand on the lower pedal
of his cycle leaned against the veranda front
and see my face, moon-stretched, in the bell
in whose forbidden ring I heard names of magic places
beyond the garden gate—Bowlalley Lane, Springhead,
Little Switzerland, Land of Green Ginger and Wincolmlee.

Sometimes I'd be allowed to meet him, just beyond
the passage-end, returning home from work, and then
he'd crook me in his arm up onto the saddle
and carry my pride high on the cycle home. I remember
the thrill of that, my impatience for the dangling legs
to grow, and the sure salt-cod smell from his coat sleeve
favouring me against the danger of a fall.

Sometimes, when he let me take his newspapers
from the saddlebag, there were sandwiches
left from lunch—made for him the previous night—
now crisped and curled at the corners,
and I'd enjoy, almost, the taste of adult fare
through a mustard-tortured tongue.

A generation later, crooking my arm and easing him
into the car, I saw anticipation light his face,
starting on a journey to countryside or shore
where we would sit and savour sandwiches and talk
of White City, Swanland, Rotenhering Staithe,
Sammy's Point and Argyle Street bridge, Gloucester Street.

GOING BACK

It seemed a good idea, going back,
not expecting to recapture heights
of summer, but to see again familiar land,
track, bridge, rowan tree and oak,
before the winter froze my will.

There comes a moment of decision,
even for a leaf.
One I watched in particular,
an oak leaf, sawing a jagged kerf
down the still sunshaft,
without farewell to siblings,
certain as the day it breached
the bud to breathe for father tree.
Now it, too, was going back
to black earth, banking roots
from which the next year's breath
would soon be starting out.

To wade through the making tide
of these decided leaves,
landlocked in a shorepool,
and contemplate my moment of decision,
it seemed a good idea, going back.

LIEBESTRAUM
(for Sylvia)

Too shy to bare to an elder sister
the reverie of boyhood, I never told;
and you would never know, playing
your prelude to the pressing day, your chords
cut records in my waking wonderment.

Yet, as your music gathered me, it was not
of the piano but of the stool I thought
recalling how, younger, I had pulled
the stool front open, plucked out
Marigold, Lavender and London Pride;
had flooded the floor with Father Thames,
Volga, Seine and Danube's blue;
had finger-raped an undreamt Liebestraum
confetti-like around the room.

How could I then have known
this haunting mattinata from the keys
was casketed betweentimes in the stool;
that voices of spring would always sing
the early morning music that you played
and spring would always bring a little hurt?

THE OTHER GRANDAD

It is the waistcoat I remember most,
and the walking-stick to ease the weight
from slow feet in bloated boots; a parcel
of dark red steak in the yellowed paper
of its day and gift-wrapped in a newspaper.
Fry it for me Maude, will you?
He shouldn't have come, I knew;
he wasn't very clean, relieved himself
at the backyard sink, and made
unpardonable noises without pardon.

Once, arriving taxied at the City Hall
fancy-dressed for the Mayoress's Ball,
we saw him propping the pillars, with his kind.
We didn't greet, just passed and went inside—
my mother a tautened string, bowed
in the orchestra of life.

I don't remember his face,
just a brown waistcoat, black-bright
between buttons; and the fat, splashed boots.

THE QUIET MEN

They boast, of deeds performed the night before,
of conquests in dark alleys of their minds,
of gallons drunk and women satisfied,
erecting pedestals and laying claims
on which to build their reputations high
in up-manship and camaraderie.

By day they learn the drills and skills of war,
defile dead ground, find trees with bushy tops
as aids to indication; march at ease,
sing ribaldry and urinate the lanes,
but never ask the question burning deep
beyond the chilling sweat, preceding sleep.

These were the quiet men before they came—
from homes like yours and mine one may suppose,
and on this battle-eve some say their prayers,
and most are virgins if the truth be told;
tomorrow there'll be taller tales to tell
and quieter men for telling them as well.

HEINZ GROPSMEYER

Almost forty years and your name still moves,
shrapnel under the skin, on reflective days.
You were not much older then than in the *Wehrmacht*
photograph above your name, twenty to my twentytwo.
Your canvas pack told more of you—*Kölnischwasser,*
talcum, *Rotbart* blades—though you had not lain
long enough to grow death's beard. More the lad
down someone's street than hated Hun or Bosch
the jackboots made of you.

I tried to pull off the boots, not to ease
your stiff feet but perhaps to please mine
or strip the camouflage from common fundamentals.
I had heard, in school, of your brown shirt,
summer camp and sung devotion to the Fatherland;
in your new fieldgrey, singing your *Horst Wessel* song
could you have heard that we, too, paraded colours
into church for blessing of the same *Gott*
you wore on your buckled belt?

And what of your comrades; he of your own age
unable to rise from his roadside splint, lifting
only his head, inches from my advancing tank,
lest the last bone of blood-let youth be crushed?
And who was he, aging, who ran through the vineyard
where Charlie took aim, life, and a sickness too?
I remember only the greylined face—and the change
in Charlie—but did not learn *his* name like yours.

Not a month later an ambulance driver
called the likes of you and me lucky
son-of-a-goddam-bitches to get up the front,
and offered to trade his Ronson for my belt that was yours.
The belt I later gave away with other spoils of war
but not your name, *Heinz Gropsmeyer,* it stayed on.
I think of us now, there where you took your *Abschied,*
green grapes under the searing *mezzogiorno* sun;
shrapnel shifting in a distant vineyard's tilth.

TAKING TOO LONG TO GO

Dying was so easy in the war—
for the young, at least;
but then, in after-mess called peace,
I saw the parbombed public library
with decayed and musty reading room
where aging men would daily sit
and slowly die.
But hygiene killed all that;
gone now the dog-eared cosiness,
replaced by glossy volumes
of glass and concrete—
a clean diaphanous mass
in open plan—denying privacy to man
with running eyes and nose
and time to sit in semi-doze
and fight his retrospective war.
His time now petrifies—a millstone weight,
time that he neither wants nor needs,
taking, like him, too long to go.

VAGRANT'S SPRING

Dog-rough
he looked,
smelt, felt;
a four-dimensional
jar to the senses.

His tears were
sprung by
primroses.

THE OLD SHIPYARD

It is silent now; the song of the yard has gone.
Only the morning ghosts of men return,
drawn through the time-clocked vortex
of their day, to witness once again
the whine to life of workshop shafting,
to wince as astringent cooling fluid
trickles at the lathe-tool's tip.
The foundry is cold where the moulders
hunched in black Saharan heat and felt
the salt sweat irrigating drum-tight skin.
Here, in the building-loft, the loftsmen sang
their fugue of scantlings—keel and turn of bilge.
These idle rolls played, then, a lively tune
when platers fashioned steel for heavy seas,
and, contrapuntal, riveters struck up
to form, from blood-red rivets, tiny Chinese hats.
The shipwright, deft with his adze as a reaper
with a swinging scythe, shaped each timber spar
as round and true as a tulip stem but stouter by far.
Wire stays and ratlines that these riggers spliced,
when set up taut and offered to the wind,
became the shantyman for many a fo'c's'le song;
and this man carving at the patternmaker's bench
was master of his craft—no Michelangelo with marble,
yet a poet in yellow pine, paring his own Pietà.

I hear them through the silence once again,
then leave the shipyard in its wrap of moss
but, sighting any ship, think of these men;
taste, in each bite of bread, their salt.

PAINTING IN PORT

What thoughts pervade their separate minds,
these two who share a swaying plank
above the wind and water line
of their rust-measled ship
and paint in shapes of foreign lands,
a red-lead archipelago from stem to stern?

Are they daubing over lives they've left
ashore in a native town whose name
would tumble strangely off my tongue
as Immingham off theirs?
Which brushmark hides nostalgia,
which patch obscures a home?

SHIP'S HUSBAND

You don't see his sort any more
except in certain well-worn streets
pushing his bow-wave against the brunt
of years, and blowing for a tug.
Tobacco smoke on his meerschaum skin
yellows the cheeks like old charts
of the sea bed, and his rusted brow
is grooved by the warps of time.
He rolls with a list to starboard
through constant drag of sea and net
and, if true to his own dictum, wears
a tarry marline amulet around his neck
against such ills as cannot be cured
by the rawness of onion or rum.
See him riding at anchor at the street end,
or berthed in an hour of sunshine
at an open sham-four door; look
through a parlour window to his past
and see his portrait—by *Jerome*—
in RNVR rig and silver frame
and always outboard-facing, moored alongside
a colour-tinted bride, netted
like a butterfly, ephemeral glamour.
She sees him now the way he was

and forgets to wind forward the clock.
But his memory fathoms greater depths,
lowering a lead-line to sound the seas
of childhood and the chanting school
whose echoing walls failed to out-shout
the sounds of the sea and crumbled
to the running tide of a schoolboy's mind.
He plumbs now the ebb-school hours
of slack-water evening, rippled
by eddies of fish-girls freed
in a clangor of clogs from the oak-chip
smokehouse, where a dozen restless cowls
once swung to the whim of the wind
and a lifetime's talk of splitting-knives,
of haddock-kits and tenterhooks.
Now, heaving in the plumb-line, he returns
to port, to fish-wife's tongue and pummice face,
her busy arms conger-strong and firm.
She, too, in her way, was a ruler of waves.

Sitting by the slipway of his season
provisioning the ship for wintry seas,
hoarfrost whitening his topmast truck, he
fears the black ice thickening his shrouds.

IRREVERENCE

There should have been no flowers.
Like goldfish gawking through a crowded bowl
these landlocked trawlers in a pool of scum
press flared bows against unyielding quay,
strain in vain to cross the concrete prison bar
from dock to river—teasing, taunting river
beckoning, with each enticing tide,
to fishing grounds now out of bounds.

There should have been a livelier wake;
no rustbound trawl-wire-hauling rollers
hanging motionless from salt-encrusted gallows,
scarred and scored but silent now
where, once, steel hawsers screamed
on brother steel, pronouncing luxury
for lucky few; flinging fingers, hands
and even life from others.

When, once, the silver fortune flashed
and slithered in the pounds on deck
and crews lent animation of their own
she rolled, pitched, yawed and was alive.
Dispersed, now, crewmen languish high and dry
while Mayweed bonnets and yellow-bobble Tansy
claim the fractured concrete quay, irreverently.
There should have been no flowers.

STRIKEBOUND

The ship's side gapes,
its unhealed wound still bare;
no caulker's tool
is spitting compressed air.
Where rustblood drips
from yet unplated frames
no pyrotechnic
welders sign their names.

A crane hook yawns
as with the wind it sways
and, metronomic,
whiles away its days.

SEASCAPE

On a day like this it seems
you could walk clear across
from one Holland to the other
without a wavelet to trip you,
and the land there like the land here
would have been deep ploughed
and disced and raked
almost as level as the sea between;
pity the sun can't see clearly
through its misting monocle
to watch my solitary ship
scratching the surface of the polished pane,
leaving a wake of powdered glass
for Neptune and a little time to smooth away,
before the sheet should crack.

GIBRALTAR POINT

Always there is surprise,
no day here a carbon copy of another.

Now the greening samphire pile
carpets the tide-swamped plain,
and a kestrel hovers the hungry sky
in wait for the bold-wandering vole.

Never the wind whispers the selfsame secret twice
to the ever-listening dunes,
decked soon in sun-scorched marram skirts,
discomforted by spines of buckthorn.

But now the gale-dried elders bow and prance
and clash their sand-lashed antlers, sensing
that the high Spring tensile sky
will shortly fill with skylark's high-flown trills.

No season's song another's carillon;
always there is surprise.

FIRST WARM DAY

First warm day of the year
and stripped of anorak and work
I walk out of winter
through April's open door
to wide expanse of shore—
where England scarfs into the sea—
and stride where early tide
has washed the dawn.

An hour, an age pass by
where shells, bereft, are left
to mark millennia or moments;
time, pace and lifepulse quicken
until, sea-air satiate,
I turn my thoughts inland again
where grounding larks embroider
footprints, lazy-daisy
in the sunsoft sand
and I, exhausted, spread
luxurious tiredness
on the outstretched beach,
lay back intoxicated head
and let the day swim in.

SOWING PEAS AND SINGING

Sowing peas and singing,
I heard a thrush chopping
the morning-brittle air into crotchets
and splintering semi-quavers
high above my own
falsetto-baritone.
At the end of one cadenza
the thrush slid off its stave
to snatch a worm
one of us had awakened—
captive treble clef
in a pincered beak; replete
the thrush excreted, delicately,
perhaps to emphasize a point,
struck up aloft, regained its higher register
and, with a farewell encore,
stilled my sowing,
killed my singing.

NIGHT DRIVE

All night I have stayed behind the wheel
repeating the broken journey of the day,
steering in a strange Welsh bed along
a now familiar reach of road, each time more slowly
than before, more light of foot and sensitive of hand,
willing the wheels' adhesion through a slape of rain.

And always, even with the camera slowing to a single frame,
the same signpost has stood its ground. The scar embarrasses,
but hides a wound as deep as that pressed on my cheek
by flaccid lips of long-forgotten aunts. At dawn,
tired and with aching arms, I yearn for the dark again,
and a changing of the film.

AT BLAENWERN

Sunday started with a buzzard trepanning
the treetops across the valley's head.
A wren sharpened its quick knife
on the bright steel of day.
In clear tones a chaffinch ministered matins
without a trace of dialect, and magpies
debated the case for black and white.

The sunlit afternoon was witnessed,
in Jehovah's name, by two young men,
one black, one white; black spoke the word
while white held the watchtower.
A rabbit plundered the private plot
and we forgave its trespass,
on Sunday at Blaenwern.

WELSH ESTUARY

Like rain from the cool Welsh hills
I had come this far.
I found the hut where he had worked,
and through the wet window
saw the crumbs of words
discarded, preserved neat
and untidy on table and floor.

Below, on the ebbed-out estuary,
a grey heron, still, on a grey day;
and above, in the graveyard,
the full rhyme of grey stones
in couplets, tercets and quatrains,
end-stopped.

And behind all this,
mocking through the mist
in which a Welshman turned
my language inside out
and back to front,
the little hill, Llareggub.
There's Welsh for you.

SLATE

Drawn from his fold on the mean mountain
the brittle man of Wales shuffles blank dominoes
and builds, on the shards of his father's dreams,
this meaner mountain, where grieving winds

polish the grim sarcophagus at Blaenau Ffestiniog.
We watch—but from a decent distance—the dismembering
of another's way of life, hewn, sawn, split and split again
to a wafer thin, then leaving the man spitting the dust

of his own drear day, well entertained we drive away
past prim rhododendron mountains, to tea and toast
on a silver tray with damask cloth at Betws-y-Coed,
and ladies with trim white hair and brown moustaches.

TREHAFOD

Let this friendly window
firelit by the evening sun
be the true beacon;
but listen well
to the smouldering language
lighting up the windows
of the cottage down the road.

(Trehafod—*Welsh*; summer home)

ON HAWORTH MOOR

Coupled in silent mist and married habit
we share the morning moor with sheep and grounded twite,
become a part of their seclusion, until a waking breeze
turns back the coverlet of cloud, and searching sun
dissolves the myth of solitude.

At Brontë Bridge we sit and watch a snake
of haversacks and walking-boots go by; warmth livens
the mood of the moor, and middle-aged men in running-strip
pant, like greyhounds, up a painful track,
chasing the fleet-foot hare of their youth.

Sheep and twite are startled by the sight of youths
with shouldered cycles, sprinting a snort of hill
to Within's Height; and now another snake, townsfolk smiling,
repeating a weekend's parole. There are more helloes
in the still of this moor than in a week of city streets.

THE DREADNOUGHT

An old boarding house by the sea, in a fog of sleep,
somewhere between bed and breakfast; no-man's hour.
The saboteur awakens, procrastinates, but knows by pressure
in the stomach's pit that the time has come for action.
He leaves, silently, not quite closing the bedroom door,
and moves, fleet as a fox, along the chill landing.
Loose boards snap like hounds at his heels. He gains
his objective, enters, sits and surveys the Dreadnought
anchored above and to his right, its chain terminating
in white porcelain with, in navy blue, the injunction "Pull".

Preliminaries duly observed, he stands to obey the command,
shatters the night with a double-clang, scuttles the Dreadnought
in a gush of sea, like a whole flotilla sinking. Exhilarated
by his guilt, he excites once more the yapping pack,
hurries to the refuge of his room, closes and bolts the door
against the noises of the night. Mission accomplished.
In bed again, fox gone to earth, he lies and contemplates
the flotsam of shipwrecked dreams in other rooms, the stretching
and groping for lights, the peerings at luminous clocks, and,
smiling between his sheets, he drowns in the depth before dawn.

PROTEST MARCH

The tree, not dressed for demonstration, streaks
its gnarled and naked limbs through city mist,
declaims no angry slogans in its cause,
but drips a silent protest on a drunk
regurgitating ale against the trunk
where mongrels sign petitions, leg by jowl.

The march approaches, banners badly spelt—
but chanted hatred needs no spelling out—
and rival voices from the gathering crowds
dispute terse invocations as they come;
mere words not proving strong enough for some,
they emphasize the dialogue with stones.

The drunk is hit, who hasn't said one word;
he adds his mark, in blood, beneath the tree
which, even as the marchers move away,
continues demonstrating underground
where dark tenacious roots, without a sound,
unnoticed, heft the man-laid flagstone path.

PENANCE AT A PIZZERIA IN LINCOLN

A paperseller presses his back to the shrubs,
lee from the chill June breeze. The cigarette
at his lips lets fall its inch of ash, and the crystal,
pendent from his nose, keeps rendezvous on the scarf
he wears like St. Patrick's cross on his chest.

Between pizza and green peppers, you can see
his placards acclaiming success at the County Show
of Charolais bulls and Lincoln Reds,
Longwool ewes and Suffolk shearling rams,
all bred by men aspiring to perfection.

Nobody's buying his papers. He moves from the shrubs
to shift his bicycle—more a crutch than conveyance—
and, perhaps to change his luck, scuffs the pavement
with inward-pointing feet on splayed, erratic legs,
immutable flogging-frame on which he represents his breed.

YOUNG MAN IN A LAY-BY

There is a fall-out here
that clouds the mind of man,
which at this time of leafthrust
does not lightly turn
to thoughts of love—
not knowing love;
here, dreams beyond this day
fly freed above the lay-by
where an engine now metes out
the beat of lifesick gas
through a pulsing plastic hose.
The laboured mind,
soon stalling,
takes its leave of life.
A car could get you
almost anywhere.

SOLO IN THREE PARTS

Indian
boy is brown and blessed
with a wheelchair, arms and hands
for manoeuvring it, and knees
to grip the cello. When the wheelchair stops
his hands tune the cello to the wind
and the strings are his voice.

Ugandan
boy is black and blessed
with ostrich legs; his arms and hands
ebony back-scratchers, just one
is strong enough to hold the begging bowl
that plays a hollow tune
and his belly is the echo.

Vietnamese
boy is blond and blessed
with a father in Wisconsin
who fought his war and went.
This child of dust holds a paper cornet
of peanuts for sale at Ho Chi Minh,
and listens for the music in the wind.

CHILD AT CHRISTMAS

He was happy with the manger,
hot breath of oxen, starfall of carols,
shepherds and simplicity.

Why did they spoil it
with red cloak of make-believe
trimmed with white lies,
bitterness of dawning truth
and loss of trust.
How long, for their sakes,
must he now pretend belief?

He didn't need the tinsel
and the trimmings.

HOLIDAY FLIGHT FROM IRAN

What to take, and what to leave behind?
It always comes to this.
But now, no ordinary holiday you plan,
standing at your season's cusp,
brooding from a storm-blown autumn window
to a winter's welcome overseas.

And now you're here; no going back this time,
no-one awaiting cards and watering plants,
only your sickened self, the earth
shaken from your shrivelled roots.
Soon, from your window in America
you gaze across to Panama and ask
yourself the question once again:
what to take, and what to leave behind.
It always comes to this.

CUCKOO

Only about once in any year
can I sling my hammock
between the greengage trunk
and apple tree, remembering
to test the non-slip knot
whose name I've quite forgotten,
stretching the canvas wide
under the fast-filling fruits,
and lie watching the shuffling leaves
piecing together a cloudless, jig-sawn sky;
or see, as now, the underbelly
of a curious thrush not long fledged
who gazes down on me; and he
may never see again such sight
as my white nest, cuckoo in his tree,
or hear, as I, from nearby dancing poplars
the swish of taffeta,
a waterfall, the sigh of one
no longer here to sigh.

BLACKBIRD HOMING

I would have chosen, rather, any other route
than meet in the dusk like this, head-on,
he swooping homeward to a hidden nest in the hedge,
I steering the country way home from my working day;
both breadwinners in our now colliding worlds.

The driving-mirror compelled a brief review,
his curtailed life in retrospect, proud plumes
which had lagged behind at birth remained
to dance in death, as though unwilling to believe
the body smashed, the strong song stilled.

Supper that night was of pasta, *maccheroni*;
on my plate, the orphaned clutch of open beaks.
At the fireside, later, in accusing dream,
a widow's silent scream.

TO MY WIFE . . .

Cloves round the ham I'd remember
and rosemary to flavour the beef.
You ask would I know how to manage
if you were the first one to die.
Manage the home? In a fashion, I'd say.
Routine? There'd be that in my life,
my goings to time and my coming back home
to find the same stillness I'd left behind
veneered with a whisper of dust.
My weekdays soothed by balsam of work.
Evenings stone-silent, only my own sad singing,
strident to reassure, just as in childhood
crossings of ghostly bedroom landings.

In our bedroom I should know cold comfort
and lonely sunbleached sheets, still
smelling the fresh-caught sea air—and you.
The bloodwarm underblanket wouldn't bring
our bed alive in love, or stilled in sleep,
and in the morning I would pour again for two,
forgetting; I'd flounder through the numbing days
to weekends' wifeless husbandry, coping,
cooking for only one reluctant appetite.
And then would be the hardest time to think,
to eat alone again, to think, and then again
the cloves round the ham I'd remember
and rosemary to flavour the beef.

SOLATIUM

It's only Sheffield plate, she would say,
but it's good and the chasing *is* by hand.
On dull afternoons she would spread old news
on the kitchen table, gather the tarnished moments
of her glinting yesterdays, upbraid them
with a gritty polish cloth blacker in parts
than her hair was grey, and I would marvel
such a dirty rag of cast-off vest
should brighten up her day so.

Stubborn pieces, like leaves on the epergne,
she'd give a harsher reprimand; verdigris
she'd even spit on, indelicately as a woman would.
Always the tray was left till last,
punished with the darkest patch of rag
and more elbow grease than all the rest,
breathed on in echo of orgasmic gasps
and titivated with the floral flannelette
of a long discarded nightdress.

After, humming a tune from Tauber, waltzing,
waiting while the kettle boiled
she would chassé the tray to the light,
mirror its gleam in her face glowing
warm where the copper showed through,
and the canary in its high sprung cage
would start again to sing.
It's only a Roller hen, she would say,
but it's company and it *has* a good song.

SONNET: THROUGH MOTHER'S EYES

In celebration of the successful cornea-grafting operation
performed, shortly after mother's death, using her eyes
in the restoration of sight to someone unknown.

An ear for music, eye for pretty sights
were gifts she'd share with anyone who cared.
She gave a rhythm to the spoken word
and lent her eyes to brighten starless nights;
she saw life's colours, not mere blacks and whites,
perceived a peacock in the plainest bird,
lit optic beacons when her joy was stirred
by children's songs or colourbox delights.

She showed her gratitude in later years,
bequeathed her eyes that others might see still,
and I'm aware, as I soliloquize,
that though my words may fail to reach her ears,
by some coincidence—and surgeon's skill—
my poem might be read through mother's eyes.

CURLEW

A heavy scent in the air of flowering may,
brassy fanfare from genista and gorse,
a chorus of foxgloves, vetch and cow parsley
hold me unready for such melancholy notes,
though your cry is as they told me it would be,
except when you savage the air with frantic gasps,
an old steam winch, the warp slipping on the whipping drum.

Sustained closehauled by the sea these many years
I've never crossed your routes, till now,
a hundred-and-sixty dry degrees across the land
from cold north-eastern ports that I call home
I see you, gaunt barred bird with a sail needle
stitching a humid canvas of Gaelic air,
reefing a headsail to the rising bowsprit of Lleyn.

WEAVER IN THE WOODS

How small am I, and yet
how huge my bursting brain.
How futile every tangled mile
inside my head
of threaded thought and plaited scheme
to braid the world my way . . .

Dwarfed, as I walk, by tall trees
the height of a hundred years,
I peer out from behind
the loom that is my mind,
seeing the woodland warder, ash,
which clusters a million sanguine keys
and accepts that few of them
will open doors to life.
Nor is it bowed by cares
for embryonic heirs.
Its neighbour, worldly oak,
writing on parchment sky,
adding to previous wills
its yearly acorn codicils,
does not care that its calligraphy
is punctuated by the pouncing breeze
now tossing teasles and goldfinches
into my eyes . . .

I breathe-in the backcloth of green . . .

and the tangled skeins unravel once again
inside the shuttle of my mind,
and the world comes woven fine
without a warp or weft of mine.

"In the beginning was the Word,
and the Word was with God, and
the Word was God" *St. John*

WORD

There is a secret in my being
that none shall know
not even you with whom
I seek to share
it tells itself so sparingly
too potent to be taken neat
root cause of all I am
enjoy and suffer
a word
I can't pronounce
yet say aloud
with every breath

Ron Harrison

MAURICE RUTHERFORD was born at Hull in 1922 and educated at the Riley High School and the College of Commerce there. He escaped from an office desk during World War Two to spend five years in the army, firstly in the Infantry and later as member of a tank crew of the IV Queen's Own Hussars in the Middle East and the Italian campaign. After the war he resumed employment in a Hull Ship Repairers' Office, crossing to the south bank of the Humber in 1961 to work as Technical Writer at Immingham Dock. Married, living at Scartho, Grimsby, he has a son and a daughter. Apart from various involvements connected with writing, he has an interest in social work and enjoys walking with his wife in the countryside.